LOVE POEMS AND
LOVE LETTERS
for all the year

With decorations by Ruth McCrea

PETER PAUPER PRESS, INC.
WHITE PLAINS · NEW YORK

To Esther and Larry
Published by:
Peter Pauper Press, Inc.
202 Mamaroneck Avenue
White Plains, NY 10601
ISBN 0-88088-417-7
Printed in Hong Kong
5   4   3

GENTLE READER

This little volume has been published in a desire to celebrate LOVE *from January to December; for true sentiment need know no single Valentine's Day, but rather should flourish and deepen each day of the year. May Cupid speed it on its journey, and St. Valentine, patron saint of lovers, bless the true in heart!*

THE PASSIONATE SHEPHERD
TO HIS LOVE

COME live with me and be my love,
And we will all the pleasures prove
That hills and valleys, dales and fields,
Or woods or steepy mountain yields.

And we will sit upon the rocks,
And see the shepherds feed their flocks
By shallow rivers, to whose falls
Melodious birds sing madrigals.

And I will make thee beds of roses
And a thousand fragrant posies;
A cap of flowers, and a kirtle
Embroider'd all with leaves of myrtle.

A gown made of the finest wool
Which from our pretty lambs we pull;
Fair-lined slippers for the cold,
With buckles of the purest gold.

A belt of straw and ivy-buds
With coral clasps and amber studs:
And if these pleasures may thee move,
Come live with me and be my love.

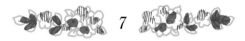

The shepherd swains shall dance and
    sing
For thy delight each May morning:
If these delights thy mind may move,
Then live with me and be my love.

CHRISTOPHER MARLOWE

KEATS TO FANNY BRAWNE

I NEVER knew before, what such love as you have made me feel, was; I did not believe in it; my Fanny was afraid of it, lest it should burn me up. But if you will fully love me, though there may be some fire 'twill not be more than we can bear when moistened and bedewed with Pleasures. . . . I love you the more in that I believe you have liked me for my own sake and for nothing else. I have met with women whom I really think would like to be married to a Poem and to be given away by a Novel. Ever yours, my love!

*   *   *   *   *

KEATS TO FANNY BRAWNE

I have no limits now to my love. I have been astonished that men could die martyrs of religion. I have shuddered at it. I shudder no more. I could be martyrd for my religion — love is my religion — I could die for you. My creed is love and you are its only tenet. You have ravish'd me away by a power I cannot resist. . . . My love is selfish. I cannot breathe without you. . . . Yours for ever.

ABSENCE

MUSIC, when soft voices die,
Vibrates in the memory;
Odors, when sweet violets sicken,
Live within the sense they quicken.

Rose leaves, when the rose is dead,
Are heap'd for the belovèd's bed;
And so thy thoughts, when thou art
    gone,
Love itself shall slumber on.

PERCY BYSSHE SHELLEY

HELEN OF TROY

Was this the face that launched a
    thousand ships?
And burnt the topless towers of Ilium?
Sweet Helen, make me immortal with
    a kiss:
Her lips suck forth my soul, see where
    it flies;
Come Helen, come give me my soul
    again.
Here will I dwell, for heaven be in
    these lips,
And all is dross that is not Helena.

CHRISTOPHER MARLOWE

SALOME

Ah, Iokanaan, Iokanaan, thou wert
the man that I love alone among men!
All other men were hateful to me.
But thou wert beautiful! Thy body
was a column of ivory set upon feet of
silver. It was a garden full of doves and
lilies of silver. It was a tower of silver
decked with shields of ivory. There was

nothing in the world so white as thy body. There was nothing in the world so black as thy hair. In the whole world there was nothing so red as thy mouth. Thy voice was a censer that scattered strange perfumes, and when I looked on thee I heard a strange music. Ah! wherefore didst thou not look at me, Iokanaan? With the cloak of thine hands, and with the cloak of thy blasphemies thou didst hide thy face. Thou didst put upon thine eyes the covering of him who would see God. Well, thou hast seen thy God, Iokanaan, but me, me, thou didst never see. If thou hadst seen me thou hadst loved me. I saw thee, and I loved thee. Oh, how I loved thee! I love thee yet, Iokanaan. I love only thee. I am athirst for thy beauty; I am hungry for thy body; and neither wine nor grapes can appease my desire. What shall I do now, Iokanaan? Neither the floods nor the great waters can quench my passion. I was a princess, and thou didst scorn me. I was a

virgin, and thou didst take my virginity from me. I was chaste, and thou didst fill my veins with fire. Ah! ah! wherefore didst thou not look at me? If thou hadst looked at me thou hadst loved me. Well I know that thou wouldst have loved me, and the mystery of Love is greater than the mystery of Death.

OSCAR WILDE

WOMAN is a miracle of divine contradictions.

JULES MICHELET

WHO ever loved, that loved not at first sight?

CHRISTOPHER MARLOWE

THE pleasure of love is in loving, and one is happier in the passion one feels than in the passion one arouses in another.

LA ROCHEFOUCAULD

March

TO ANTHEA,
WHO MAY COMMAND
HIM ANYTHING

Bɪᴅ me to live, and I will live
 Thy Protestant to be;
Or bid me love, and I will give
 A loving heart to thee.

A heart as soft, a heart as kind,
 A heart as sound and free
As in the whole world thou canst find,
 That heart I'll give to thee.

Bid that heart stay, and it will stay
 To honor thy decree:
Or bid it languish quite away,
 And 't shall do so for thee.

Bid me to weep, and I will weep
 While I have eyes to see:
And, having none, yet will I keep
 A heart to weep for thee.

Bid me despair; and I'll despair
 Under that cypress-tree:

Or bid me die, and I will dare
   E'en death to die for thee.

Thou art my life, my love, my heart,
   The very eyes of me:
And hast command of every part
   To live and die for thee.

ROBERT HERRICK

LUDWIG VAN BEETHOVEN TO THE "IMMORTAL BELOVED"

GOOD MORNING

THOUGH still in bed my thoughts go out to you, my Immortal Beloved, now and then joyfully, then sadly, waiting to learn whether or not fate will hear us. I can live only wholly with you or not at all — yes, I am resolved to wander so long away from you until I can fly to your arms and say that I am really at home, send my soul enwrapped in you into the land of spirits. — Yes, unhappily it must be so — you will be the more resolved since you know my fidel-

ity — to you, no one can ever again possess my heart — none — never — Oh, God! why is it necessary to part from one whom one so loves and yet my life in W. [Vienna] is now a wretched life — your love makes me at once the happiest and the unhappiest of men — at my age, I need a steady, quiet life — can that be under our conditions? My angel, I have just been told that the mail coach goes every day — and I must close at once so that you may receive the L. at once. Be calm, only by a calm consideration of our existence can we achieve our purpose to live together — be calm — love me — today — yesterday — what tearful longings for you — you — you — my life — my all — farewell — Oh continue to love me — never misjudge the most faithful heart of

your beloved L.

ever thine

ever mine

ever for each other.

ROMANCE

I WILL make you brooches and toys for
    your delight
Of birdsong at morning and starshine
    at night
I will make a palace fit for you and me
Of green days in forests and blue days
    at sea.

I will make my kitchen and you shall
    keep your room
Where white flows the river and bright
    blows the broom,
And you shall wash your linen and
    keep your body white
In rainfall at morning and dewfall at
    night.

And this shall be for music when no
    one else is near,
The fine song for singing, the rare song
    to hear!
That only I remember, that only you
    admire,

Of the broad road that stretches and
   the roadside fire.

ROBERT LOUIS STEVENSON

MY LOVE'S A MATCH

MY LOVE's a match in beauty
   For every flower that blows,
Her little ear's a lily,
   Her velvet cheek a rose;
Her locks like gilly gowans
   Hang golden to her knee.
If I were King of Ireland,
   My Queen she'd surely be.

Her eyes are fond forget-me-nots,
   And no such snow is seen
Upon the heaving hawthorn bush
   As crests her bodice green.
The thrushes when she's talking
   Sit listening on the tree.
If I were King of Ireland,
   My Queen she'd surely be.

ALFRED P. GRAVES

ONE WORD

ONE word is too often profaned
    For me to profane it;
One feeling too falsely disdained
    For thee to disdain it;
One hope is too like despair
    For prudence to smother;
And pity from thee more dear
    Than that from another.

I can give not what men call love:
    But wilt thou accept not
The worship the heart lifts above
    And the heavens reject not,
The desire of the moth for the star,
    Of the night for the morrow,
The devotion to something afar
    From the sphere of our sorrow?

PERCY BYSSHE SHELLEY

PLEASURE has its time; so, too, has wisdom. Make love in thy youth, and in old age attend to thy salvation.

VOLTAIRE

DAPHNIS AND CHLOE

When they returned to the fields next day, while Daphnis sat under the oak, as his custom was, playing his flute as the she-goats lay about him, Chloe sat by him, watching her ewes grazing; but more often still her eyes were turned from them to Daphnis. And finding him beautiful, and thinking his beauty might come from the music, she took the flute from him and played it herself, that she might be as beautiful as he.

Then she urged him to bathe once more, and while he bathed she saw him naked and was unable to resist touching him. And when they returned homeward in the evening she still thought of Daphnis naked, and this thought was the beginning of her love. And soon she had no thoughts and no dreamings of anything except Daphnis, and never spoke of anything but him. What she felt she could not find words to tell, for she was only a simple girl reared in the fields, and never in her life had ever heard the word: love. All the same, her soul was heavy, and very often her eyes filled with tears. Days passed without her enjoying any food and nights without her finding sleep. She laughed, and while she laughed, tears fell. She slept, and a moment after was awake and sitting up on her pallet. She grew pale, and then her face was aflame. The heifer stung by the fly was never madder than she. She would fall at times into a reverie, and while all alone she talked to herself in this fashion:

I am sick, but I do not know what my sickness is. I hurt, but there is no wound. I mourn, yet no sheep is dead. I burn, even in coolest shade. Many briars have scratched me, but I did not weep, nor have I cried when stung by bees. Therefore this sickness that fills my heart must be more dangerous than any I have had before. True it is that Daphnis is beautiful; but he is not the

only one. His cheeks are red, but flow-ers are, too. He sings, but the birds do too. And yet when I see the flowers and hear the birds, they do not leave me with any pain. Oh, that I were his flute, and he might put me to his lips! Oh, that I were a little kid, and he might take me in his arms! Oh, cruel fountain whose waters have made him so beau-tiful, can you not make me beautiful, too? Oh nymphs, you will not let me die, I who was born and lived among you? Who then after me would weave you garlands and nosegays? And who will care for my poor lambs? And my pretty cricket, that I had such trouble to catch, how useless your song will be in the hot noontide! Your voice can not longer bring sweet sleep to me under the branches. Daphnis has robbed me of sleep.

So did the girl speak, all a-wonder within herself at what had befallen her, consumed by a fire but unable to put a name to it.

LONGUS

GATHER YE ROSEBUDS

GATHER ye rosebuds while ye may,
    Old Time is still a-flying;
And this same flower that smiles today
    Tomorrow will be dying.

The glorious lamp of heaven, the Sun,
    The higher he's a-getting,
The sooner will his race be run,
    And nearer he's to setting.

That age is best, which is the first,
    When youth and blood are warmer
But being spent, the worse, and worst
    Times still succeed the former.

Then be not coy, but use your time,
    And while you may, go marry:
For having lost but once your prime,
    You may for ever tarry.

ROBERT HERRICK

IT IS the woman who chooses the man
who will choose her.

PAUL GERALDY

LOVE

THE introduction to this felicity is in private and tender relation of one to one, which is the enchantment of human life; which, like a certain divine rage and enthusiasm, seizes on man at one period and works a revolution in his mind and body; unites him to his race, pledges him to the domestic and civic relations, carries him with new sympathy into nature, enhances the power of the senses, opens the imagination, adds to his character heroic and sacred attributes, establishes marriage and gives permanence to human society.

RALPH WALDO EMERSON

RUBAIYAT OF OMAR KHAYYAM

ALAS, that Spring should vanish with
    the Rose!
That Youth's sweet-scented manuscript
    should close!

THE Nightingale that in the branches
    sang,
Ah, whence, and whither flown again,
    who knows!
Ah Love! could thou and I with Fate
    conspire
To grasp this sorry Scheme of Things
    entire,
Would not we shatter it to bits and
    then
Re-mould it nearer to the Heart's
    Desire?

EDWARD FITZGERALD

LOVE is the burden of all nature's odes;
the song of the birds is an epithala-
mium, a hymeneal. The marriage of
the flowers spots the meadows and
fringes the hedges with pearls and dia-
monds. In the deep waters, in the high
air, in woods and pastures, and the
bowels of the earth, this is the employ-
ment and condition of all things.

HENRY THOREAU

HOW DO I LOVE THEE?

How do I love thee? Let me count the
    ways.
I love thee to the depth and breadth
    and height
My soul can reach, when feeling out
    of sight
For the ends of Being and ideal Grace.
I love thee to the level of every day's
Most quiet need, by sun and candle-
    light.
I love thee freely, as men strive for Right;
I love thee purely, as they turn from
    Praise.
I love thee with the passion put to use
In my old griefs, and with my child-
    hood's faith.
I love thee with a love I seemed to lose
With my lost saints, — I love thee with
    the breath,
Smiles, tears, of all my life! — and, if
    God choose,
I shall but love thee better after death.

ELIZABETH BARRETT BROWNING

SWEET, CAN I SING

SWEET, can I sing you the song of your
    kisses?
How soft is this one, how subtle this is,
How fluttering swift as a bird's kiss
    that is,
As a bird that taps at a leafy lattice;
How this one clings and how that
    uncloses
From bud to flowers in the way of roses;
And this through laughter and that
    through weeping
Swims to the brim where Love lies
    sleeping;
And this in a point I snatch, and capture
That in the ecstasy of rapture,
When the odorous red-rose petals part
That my lips may find their way to the
    heart
Of the rose of the world, your lips, my
    rose.
But no song knows
The way of my heart to the heart of my
    rose.   ARTHUR SYMONS

HENRY VIII TO ANNE BOLEYN

MYNE awne Sweetheart, this shall be
to advertise you of the great ellingness*
that I find here since your departing,
for I ensure you, me thinketh the Tyme
longer since your departing now last
than I was wont to do a whole Fort-
night; I think your Kindness and my
Fervence of Love causeth it, for other-
wise I wolde not thought it possible,
that for so little a while it should have
grieved me, but now that I am come-
ing toward you, me thinketh my Pains
by half released, and also I am right
well comforted, insomuch that my
Book maketh substantially for my Mat-
ter, in writing whereof I have spent
above IIII Hours this Day, which
caused me now write the shorter Letter to you at this Tyme, because of some
Payne in my Head, wishing my self
(specially an Evening) in my Sweet-
hearts Armes whose pritty Duckys I

* Loneliness

trust shortly to kysse. Writne with the
Hand of him that was, is, and shall be
yours by his will,

H. R.

A RED, RED ROSE

My Luve's like a red, red rose
    That's newly sprung in June:
O my Luve's like the melodie
    That's sweetly play'd in tune!

As fair art thou, my bonnie lass,
    So deep in luve am I:
And I will luve thee still, my dear,
    Till a' the seas gang dry:

Till a' the seas gang dry, my dear,
    And the rocks melt wi' the sun;
I will luve thee still, my dear,
    While the sands o' life shall run.

And fare thee weel, my only Luve,
    And fare thee weel a while!
And I will come again, my Luve,
    Tho' it were ten thousand mile.

ROBERT BURNS

A STOLEN KISS

Now GENTLE sleep hath closèd up those
    eyes
Which, waking, kept my boldest
    thoughts in awe;
And free access unto that sweet lip lies,
From whence I long the rosy breath to
    draw.

Methinks no wrong it were, if I should
    steal
From those two melting rubies one
    poor kiss;
None sees the theft that would the
    theft reveal,
Nor rob I her of aught that she can
    miss;

Nay, should I twenty kisses take away,
There would be little sign I would do
    so;
Why then should I this robbery delay?
O, she may wake, and therewith angry
    grow!

Well, if she do, I'll back restore that
    one,
And twenty hundred thousand more
    for loan.

GEORGE WITHER

LOVE'S PHILOSOPHY

THE fountains mingle with the river,
    And the rivers with the Ocean,
The winds of Heaven mix for ever
    With a sweet emotion;
Nothing in the world is single:
    All things by a law divine
In one spirit meet and mingle.
    Why not I with thine?

See the mountains kiss high Heaven
    And the waves clasp one another;
No sister flower would be forgiven
    If it disdained its brother;
And the sunlight clasps the earth
    And the moonbeams kiss the sea;
What is all this sweet work worth
    If thou kiss not me?

PERCY BYSSHE SHELLEY

WHEN A BELOVÈD HAND

WHEN a belovèd hand is laid in ours,
When, jaded with the rush and glare
Of the interminable hours,
Our eyes can in another's eyes read
    clear,
When our world-deafened ear
Is by the tones of a loved voice
    caressed, —
A bolt is shot back somewhere in our
    breast,
And a lost pulse of feeling stirs again.
The eye sinks inward, and the heart
    lies plain,
And what we mean, we say, and what
    we would, we know!
A man becomes aware of his life's flow,
And hears its winding murmur, and
    he sees
The meadows where it glides, the sun,
    the breeze
And there arrives a lull in the hot race,
Wherein he doth for ever chase
That flying and elusive shadow, rest.

An air of coolness plays upon his face,
And an unwonted calm pervades his
    breast.
And then he thinks he knows
The hills where his life rose,
And the sea where it goes.

MATTHEW ARNOLD

JUNE

Last June I saw your face three times,
   Three times I touched your hand;
Now, as before, May month is o'er,
   And June is in the land.

O many Junes shall come and go,
   Flower-footed o'er the mead;
O many Junes for me, to whom
   Is length of days decreed.

There shall be sunlight, scent of rose,
   Warm mist of Summer rain;
Only this change — I shall not look
   Upon your face again.

AMY LEVY

BYRON TO THE
COUNTESS GUICCIOLI

MY DEAREST TERESA, — I have read this
book in your garden; — my love, you
were absent, or else I could not have
read it. It is a favorite book of yours,
and the writer was a friend of mine.
You will not understand these English
words, and *others* will not understand
them, — which is the reason I have not
scrawled them in Italian. But you will
recognize the handwriting of him who
passionately loved you, and you will
divine that, over a book which was
yours, he could only think of love.

In that word, beautiful in all lan-
guages, but most so in yours — *Amor
mio* — is comprised my existence here
and hereafter. I feel I exist here, and I
feel that I shall exist hereafter, — to
what purpose you will decide; my des-
tiny rests with you, and you are a
woman, eighteen years of age, and two
out of a convent. I wish that you had

staid there, with all my heart, — or, at least, that I had never met you in your married state.

But all this is too late. I love you, and you love me, — at least, you *say* so, and *act* as if you *did* so, which last is a great consolation in all events. But *I* more than love you, and cannot cease to love you.

Think of me, sometimes, when the Alps and ocean divide us, — but they never will, unless you *wish* it.

WOMAN

When lovely woman stoops to folly,
　And finds too late that men betray,
What charm can soothe her melan-
　　choly?
　What art can wash her tears away?

The only art her guilt to cover,
　To hide her shame from ev'ry eye,
To give repentance to her lover,
　And wring his bosom is — to die.

OLIVER GOLDSMITH

DESTINY

Somewhere there waiteth in this
    world of ours
For one lone soul another lonely soul,
Each choosing each through all the
    weary hours
And meeting strangely at one sudden
    goal.
Then blend they, like green leaves
    with golden flowers,
Into one beautiful and perfect whole;
And life's long night is ended, and the
    way
Lies open onward to eternal day.

EDWIN ARNOLD

It is better to be silent than to say
things at the wrong time that are too
tender; what was appropriate ten sec-
onds ago is so no longer, and hurts one's
cause, rather than helps it.

STENDHAL

WE'LL GO NO MORE

So, we'll go no more a-roving
    So late into the night,
Though the heart be still as loving,
    And the moon be still as bright.

For the sword outwears its sheath,
    And the soul wears out the breast,
And the heart must pause to breathe,
    And love itself have rest.

Though the night was made for loving,
    And the day returns too soon,
Yet we'll go no more a-roving
    By the light of the moon.

LORD BYRON

BROWNING TO ELIZABETH BAR-RETT AFTER THEIR MARRIAGE

You will only expect a few words —
what will those be? When the heart is
full it may run over, but the real full-
ness stays within.

You asked me yesterday "if I should
repent?" Yes — my own Ba, — I could

wish all the past were to do over again, that in it I might somewhat more, — never so little more, conform in the outward homage, to the inward feeling. What I have professed . . . (for I have performed nothing) seems to fall short of what my first love required even — and when I think of this moment's love . . . I could repent, as I say. Words can never tell you, however, — form them, transform them any way, how perfectly dear you are to me — perfectly dear to my heart and soul.

I look back, and in every one point, every word and every gesture, every letter, every silence — you have been entirely perfect to me — I would not change one word, one look.

My hope and aim are to preserve this love, not to fall from it — for which I trust to God who procured it for me, and doubtless can preserve it.

Enough now, my dearest, dearest, own Ba! You have given me the highest, completest proof of love that ever

one human being gave another. I am all gratitude — and all pride (under the proper feeling which ascribes pride to the right source) all pride that my life has been so crowned by you.

God bless you prays your very own R.

ONE-AND-TWENTY

WHEN I was one-and-twenty
  I heard a wise man say,
"Give crowns and pounds and guineas
  But not your heart away;
Give pearls away and rubies
  But keep your fancy free."
But I was one-and-twenty,
  No use to talk to me.
When I was one-and-twenty
  I heard him say again,
"The heart out of the bosom
  Was never given in vain;
'Tis paid with sighs a-plenty
  And sold for endless rue."
And I am two-and-twenty,
  And oh, 'tis true, 'tis true!

A. E. HOUSMAN

September

THERE IS A LADY

THERE is a Lady sweet and kind,
Was never face so pleased my mind;
I did but see her passing by,
And yet I love her till I die.

Her gesture, motion, and her smiles
Her wit, her voice my heart beguiles,
Beguiles my heart, I know not why,
And yet I love her till I die.

Cupid is wingèd and doth range
Her country so my love doth change:
But change she earth, or change she
    sky,
Yet will I love her till I die.

ANONYMOUS

THE plain English of the politest ad-
dress of a gentleman to lady, is, I am
now, dear madam, the humblest of
your servants: Be so good as to allow
me to be your Lord and Master.

SAMUEL RICHARDSON

TO HIS COY MISTRESS

HAD we but world enough, and time,
This coyness, Lady, were no crime.
We would sit down and think which
    way
To walk and pass our long love's day.
Thou by the Indian Ganges' side
Shouldst rubies find: I by the tide
Of Humber would complain. I would
Love you ten years before the Flood,
And you should, if you please, refuse
Till the conversion of the Jews.
My vegetable love should grow
Vaster than empires, and more slow;
An hundred years should go to praise
Thine eyes and on thy forehead gaze;
Two hundred to adore each breast,
But thirty thousand to the rest;
An age at least to every part,
And the last age should show your heart.
For, Lady, you deserve this state,
Nor would I love at lower rate.

But at my back I always hear
Time's wingèd chariot hurrying near;

And yonder all before us lie
Deserts of vast eternity.
Thy beauty shall no more be found,
Nor, in thy marble vault, shall sound
My echoing song: then worms shall try
That long preserved virginity,
And your quaint honor turn to dust,
And into ashes all my lust:
The grave's a fine and private place,
But none, I think, do there embrace.

Now therefore, while the youthful hue
Sits on thy skin like morning dew,
And while thy willing soul transpires
At every port with instant fires,
Now let us sport us while we may,
And now, like amorous birds of prey,
Rather at once our time devour
Than languish in his slow-chapt power.
Let us roll all our strength and all
Our sweetness up into one ball,
And tear our pleasures with rough strife
Through the iron gates of life:
Thus, though we cannot make our sun
Stand still, yet we will make him run.

ANDREW MARVELL

WHEN I THINK

BELOVÈD, my Belovèd, when I think
That thou wast in the world a year ago,
What time I sat alone here in the snow
And saw no footprint, heard the silence
        sink
No moment at thy voice, . . . but, link by
        link,
When counting all my chains, as if that so
They never could fall off at any blow
Struck by thy possible hand . . . why,
        thus I drink
Of life's great cup of wonder!
        Wonderful
Never to feel thee thrill the day or night
With personal act or speech — nor ever
        cull
Some prescience of thee with the
        blossoms white
Thou sawest growing! Atheists are as
        dull
Who cannot guess God's presence out
        of sight.

ELIZABETH BARRETT BROWNING

Love, at first sight, supposes such a susceptibility of passion, as, however it may pass in a man, very little becomes the delicacy of the female character.

SAMUEL RICHARDSON

NELSON TO LADY HAMILTON

"Victory," October 19th, 1805

My dearest Beloved Emma, the dear friend of my bosom. The signal has been made that the enemy's combined fleet are coming out of the port. We have very little wind, so that I have no hopes of seeing them before tomorrow. May the God of battles crown my endeavors with success; at all events, I will take care that my name shall ever be most dear to you and Horatio, both of whom I love as much as my own life. And as my last writing, before the battle, will be to you, so I hope, in God, that I shall live to finish my letter after the battle. May heaven bless you, prays your

NELSON

I LOVE HIM

I LOVE him, I dream of him,
    I sing of him by day;
And all the night I hear him talk, —
    And yet he's far away.

There's beauty in the morning,
    There's sweetness in the May,
There's music in the running stream;
    And yet he's far away.

I love him, I trust in him;
    He trusteth me alway:
And so the time flies hopefully,
    Although he's far away.

BARRY CORNWALL

DE L'AMOUR

SHE leaves you because she is too sure of you. You killed fear, and the little doubts of happy love can no longer be born; disquiet her and, above all, keep yourself from the absurdity of making protestations.

STENDHAL

November

NAPOLEON TO JOSEPHINE

I DON'T love you, not at all; on the contrary, I detest you — You're a naughty, gawky, foolish Cinderella. You never write me; you don't love your husband; you know what pleasure your letters give him, and yet you haven't written him six lines, dashed off casually!

What do you do all day, Madam? What is the affair so important as to leave you no time to write to your devoted lover? What affection stifles and puts to one side the love, the tender and constant love you promised him? Of what sort can be that marvelous being, that new lover who absorbs every moment, tyrannizes over your days, and prevents your giving any attention to your husband? Josephine, take care! Some fine night, the doors will be broken open, and there I'll be.

Indeed, I am very uneasy, my love, at receiving no news of you; write me quickly four pages, pages full of agree-

able things which shall fill my heart with the pleasantest feelings.

I hope before long to crush you in my arms and cover you with a million kisses burning as though beneath the equator.

BONAPARTE

IN A GONDOLA

THE moth's kiss, first!
Kiss me as if you made believe
You were not sure, this eve,
How my face, your flower, had pursed
Its petals up; so, here and there
You brush it, till I grow aware
Who wants me, and wide ope I burst.

The bee's kiss, now!
Kiss me as if you enter'd gay
My heart at some noonday,
A bud that dares not disallow
The claim, so all is render'd up,
And passively its shatter'd cup
Over your head to sleep I bow.

ROBERT BROWNING

AUCASSIN AND NICOLETE

WHEN Aucassin heard Nicolete say that she would pass into a far country, he was all in wrath.

"Fair sweet friend," quoth he, "thou shalt not go, for then wouldst be my death. And the first man that saw thee and had the might withal, would take thee straightway into his bed to be his leman. And once thou camest into a man's bed, and that bed not mine, wit ye well that I would not tarry till I had found a knife to pierce my heart and slay myself. Nay, verily, wait so long I would not: but would hurl myself on it soon as I could find a wall, or a black stone, thereon would I dash my head so mightily, that the eyes would start, and my brain burst. Rather would I die even such a death, than know thou hadst lain in a man's bed, and that bed not mine."

ANONYMOUS

December

SONG

Nay! if thou must depart, thou shalt
    depart;
But why so soon — oh, heart-blood of
    my heart?
Go then! yet — going — turn and stay
    thy feet,
That I may once more see that face so
    sweet.
Once more — if never more; for swift
    days go
As hastening waters from their
    fountains flow;
And whether yet again shall meeting
    be
Who knows? Who knows? Ah! turn
    once more to me!

EDWIN ARNOLD

Absence lessens half-hearted passions,
and increases great ones, as the wind
puts out the candle and yet stirs up the
fire.

LA ROCHEFOUCAULD

MANON LESCAUT

WE SAT down side by side. I took her hand in mine. Ah Manon! said I, gazing at her with sad eyes, I had not a thought of the black treachery with which you repaid my love. It was easy for you to deceive a heart of which you were absolute sovereign, and whose whole happiness was set in pleasing and obeying you. Tell me, have you found any since as tender and as submissive? No, no. Nature will hardly have made another of the same temper. Tell me at least if you have sometimes regretted it? What am I to count on in this return of tenderness that brings you here to comfort me? I see only too well that you are lovelier than ever: but in the name of all the grief that I have suffered from you, tell me, lovely Manon, if you will be more faithful?

She made answer, telling me such touching things of her repentance, and bound herself to constancy with so

many vows and protestations, that she softened me beyond my saying. Dearest Manon, I cried, profanely mingling the language of Love and Theology, you are too adorable for a created thing. I feel my heart swept by an overpowering delight.

ABBE PREVOST

SONG

FILL the swift days full, my dear,
    Since life is fleet;
Love, and hold Love fast, my dear,
    He is so sweet —
Sweetest, dearest, fleetest comer,
Fledgling of the sudden summer.

Love, but not too well, my dear!
    When skies are gray,
And the autumn winds are here,
    Love will away —
Fleetest, vaguest, farthest rover,
When the summer's warmth is over.

LOUISE MOULTON

AS A PERFUME

As A perfume doth remain
In the folds where it hath lain,
So the thought of you, remaining
Deeply folded in my brain,
Will not leave me: all things leave me:
   You remain.

Other thoughts may come and go,
Other moments I may know
That shall waft me, in their going,
As a breath blown to and fro,
Fragrant memories: fragrant memories
   Come and go.

Only thoughts of you remain
In my heart where they have lain,
Perfumed thoughts of you, remaining,
A hid sweetness, in my brain.
Others leave me: all things leave me:
   You remain.

ARTHUR SYMONS